This book says a lot of things I'd like you to hold close to your heart forever.

But most of all, I want it to remind you, in all the days to come...

You have your whole life ahead of you, and I want it to be a wonderful one.

Author's acknowledgments: To begin with, I want to express my love and thanks to my sons. Being the father of two amazing teenagers (one current, one former) has been the experience of a lifetime, and I wouldn't have missed it for the world. Jordan and Casey, I hope that — in some way — I have inspired you. I am certain that — in many ways — you have been an inspiration to me. Thanks also to Colorado artist Kristin Sheldon. I have been a fan of her work for many years, and it's great to be able to include some of her wonderful, whimsical designs on these pages. And finally, as always… a huge note of gratitude to all the terrific people at Blue Mountain Arts, for everything they do so well.

All writings are by Douglas Pagels except as noted.

Library of Congress Control Number: 2005921115
ISBN: 0-88396-926-2

Certain trademarks are used under license.
BLUE MOUNTAIN PRESS is registered in U.S. Patent and Trademark Office.

Manufactured in the United States of America.
First Printing: 2005

❀ This book is printed on recycled paper

This book is printed on fine quality, laid embossed, 80 lb. paper. This paper has been specially produced to be acid free (neutral pH) and contains no groundwood or unbleached pulp. It conforms with the requirements of the American National Standards Institute, Inc., so as to ensure that this book will last and be enjoyed by future generations.

Blue Mountain Arts, Inc.

P.O. Box 4549, Boulder, Colorado 80306

Required Reading
for All
Teenagers

(Or at least for
one who is very
important
to me!)

Douglas Pagels

Illustrated by Kristin Sheldon

Blue Mountain Press™
Boulder, Colorado

Featured Authors

Michael Jordan

Mia Hamm

Lance Armstrong

R. L. Evans

Clay Aiken

Thomas Huxley

Venus Williams

Picabo Street

Brandi Chastain

Serena Williams

Confucius

Mariel Hemingway

Terrell Owens

Thomas A. Edison

Patti LaBelle

Contents

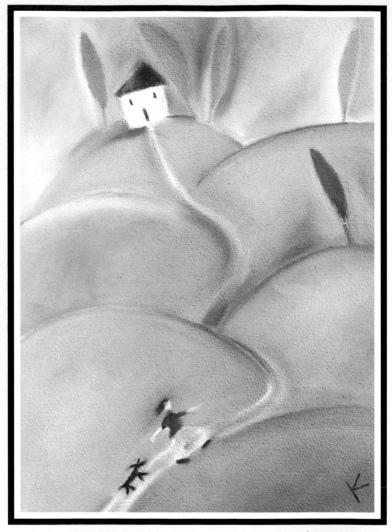

The Road Home

*I want you to know
that one of the most
important things
in this world
is your presence in it.*

Required Reading

Has anyone told you lately... what a wonderful person you are?

I hope so! I hope you've been told dozens of times... because you are just amazing. And in case you haven't heard those words in awhile, I want you to hear them now. You deserve to know that...

It takes someone special to do what you do. It takes someone rare and remarkable to make the lives of everyone around them so much nicer. It takes someone everyone can be proud of... a youthful soul who is learning and growing and going toward the horizons that lie ahead. It takes someone who is living proof of how precious a person can be.

It takes someone... just like you.

Words to Help You Be Strong
Along the Path of Life

I can barely begin to tell you of all my wishes for you ■ There are so many of them, and I want them all to come true ■ I want you to use your heart as a compass as you grow and find your way in the world, but I want you to always have an appreciation for the direction of home ■ I want you to have self-esteem and self-confidence and to be self-sufficient, but also to know that you will never be alone ■ I want you to be safe and smart and cautious ■ I want you to be wise beyond your years ■ I don't want you to grow up too fast ■ I want you to come to me with your fears ■ I want the people who share your days to realize that they are in the presence of a very special someone ■ You are a wonderful, rare person with no comparison ■

I want you to know that opportunities will come, and you'll have many goals to achieve ■ The more that obstacles get in the way of your dreams, the more you'll need to believe ■ Get your feet wet with new experiences, but be sure you never get in over your head ■ I want you to realize how capable you are and that your possibilities are unlimited ■ I hope you never lose your childlike wonder, your delight and appreciation in interesting things ■ I know you'll keep responding in a positive way to the challenges life always brings ■ I want you to set the stage for living in a way that reflects good choices and a great attitude ■ I want you to honor... the wonder of you ■

I have created the opportunity to have a choice. That is how I am going to live.
— *Michael Jordan*

Skating at the Pond

One of the most important parts of being a winner in life is being happy. A happy person makes those around them happy as well, and that is one of the greatest gifts of all. Make decisions in your life that lead to happiness.

— Mia Hamm

Be Yourself

Hold on to your dreams, and never let them
go ■ Show the world how wonderful you are ■
Wish on a star that shines in your sky ■ Rely
on all the strength you have inside ■ Stay in
touch with those who touch your life with love ■
Look on the bright side and don't let adversity
keep you from winning ■ Be yourself, because
you are filled with special qualities that have
brought you this far, and that will always see
you through ■ Keep your spirits up ■ Make
your heart happy, and let it reflect on everything
you do!

A Reason to Smile

I want you to know how amazing you are.
I want you to know how much you're
treasured and celebrated and quietly thanked.

I want you to feel really good...
   about who you are.
About all the great things you do!
I want you to appreciate your uniqueness.
Acknowledge your talents and abilities.
Understand the wonder within.

You make so much sun shine through, and you inspire so much joy in the lives of everyone who is lucky enough to know you.

You are so special, giving so many people a reason to smile. You deserve to receive the best in return, and one of my heart's favorite hopes is that the happiness you give away will come back to warm you
each and every day of your life.

I want you to have as much happiness as tomorrow can promise to anyone.

Bikes Around Town

Remember: it's all about choices.
Realize: the decisions are up to you.
And don't forget: you're in the driver's seat, and you
can travel through life in any direction you choose.

It's Pretty Much Up to You

Decisions are incredibly important things!
Good decisions will come back to bless you.
Bad decisions can come back to haunt you.

That's why it's so important that you take the
time to choose wisely. Choose to do the things
that reflect well… on your ability, your integrity,
your spirit, your health, your tomorrows, your
smiles, your dreams, and yourself.

You are such a wonder. You're the only one in
the universe exactly like you! I want you to take
care of that rare and remarkable soul. I want you
to know that there is someone who will thank
you for doing the things you do now with
foresight and wisdom and respect.

It's the person you will someday be. You have a
chance to make that person so thankful and so
proud. All you have to do is remember one of
the lessons I learned when I made a similar
journey. It's pretty simple, really; just these
eight words:

> Each time you're given the chance…
> choose wisely.

Teens Have It Tough

There was social pressure at (my high school), but my mother and I couldn't begin to keep up with the Joneses, so we didn't even try....

I felt shunned at times. I was the guy who did weird sports and who didn't wear the right labels.

— Lance Armstrong

> Don't let life discourage you; everyone who got where he is had to begin where he was.
> — R. L. Evans

So much has happened since *American Idol*....
I... wanted to share stories about my life in the hope that it might enable a handful of other people to feel better about themselves.

I was dubbed a loser throughout most of my childhood. As a kid, I was an insult magnet — a nerd who loved his grandparents, who wore the wrong clothes, who liked the wrong things, who had goofy hair and glasses, who didn't smoke or drink.

It made for a lonely childhood. More than a decade later, I figured out that the real reason people didn't like me was that *I* didn't like me. When I learned to believe in myself, to have faith and to remain stubborn in my convictions, my life changed. Once I decided I was okay, other people agreed. And those folks who didn't agree didn't matter so much anymore....

By senior year, I was just as popular as anybody else... I had gone from being school bottom-feeder to being one of the most well-liked students in school. It was surreal.

My recognition had nothing to do with anything external. My mama still wouldn't buy me nice clothes. I still had big old glasses and hair that nothing could be done with... I was still skinny and uncoordinated.

The only thing different about me was how I felt about myself.

— Clay Aiken

Checking Out That Person in the Mirror

You are something — and someone — very special. You really are. No one else in this entire world is exactly like you, and there are so many incredible things about you.

You're a one-of-a-kind treasure, uniquely here in this space and time. You are here to shine in your own wonderful way, sharing your smile in the best way you can, and remembering all the while that a little light somewhere makes a brighter light everywhere. You can — and you do — make a wonderful contribution to this world.

You have qualities within you that many people would love to have, and those who really and truly know you… are so glad that they do. You have a big heart and a good and sensitive soul. You are gifted with thoughts and ways of seeing things that only special people know. You know that life doesn't always play by the rules, but that in the long run, everything will work out.

You understand that you and your actions
are capable of turning anything around —
and that joys once lost can always be found.
There is a resolve and an inner reserve of
strength in you that few ever get to see.
You have so many treasures within — those
you're only beginning to discover, and all
the ones you're already aware of.

Never forget what a treasure you are. That
special person in the mirror may not always
get to hear all the compliments you
deserve, but
   you are so worthy of
     such an abundance
       ...of friendship, joy, and love.

> *You're an original, an*
> *individual, a masterpiece.*
> *Celebrate that; don't let your*
> *uniqueness make you shy.*

You've got a big heart. Keep it filled with happiness. You've got a fascinating mind. Keep finding new ways to grow.

Keep trying. Keep smiling. Keep yearning. Keep learning.

Try to learn something about everything and everything about something.
— *Thomas Huxley*

Hitting the Books

Serena and I believe there's nothing more important in life than getting a good education. We want you to become so determined to learn that you don't allow anyone or anything to come between you and your schoolwork....

The people and conditions in your life change from day to day. But the things you learn will always stay with you. Knowledge is the one thing that no one can take away from you — ever, no matter what. This is really important for you to understand.... The more you learn, the better your future will be and the more choices you'll have.

— Venus Williams

Artist's Point

Get... involved in as many activities as possible.
Try everything: sports, music, art... choir... drama....
You never know where you're going to find your niche.
I found mine, and it changed my life.

— *Picabo Street*

Desired Reading

If you've been asked once, you've probably been asked a thousand times: "What do you want to be when you grow up?" The best answer I ever heard came from an anonymous third-grader who replied, "I would like to be myself. I tried to be other things, but I always failed."

Being yourself will lead you to a better understanding of your hopes and goals and desires and dreams. Being in tune with who you are and what you like helps you with answering the question: how do you find your calling in life?

The good news is: you don't have to. (At least not yet!) The even better news is, your calling will probably find you. Sometimes you don't know what you desire until you get a taste of it. You've had that scenario play itself out many times in your life. You didn't know you liked this music, that food, this sport, etc… until you tried it. And once you made the discovery, you could plainly see that the two of you were meant to be.

If the answer to life's big question is, "I don't know what I want to be," maybe it's just because you haven't stumbled across the right role model or awesome class or inspiring experience yet. But… if there is one subject that shines so bright that it makes you wish you could spend more of your life in pursuit of it, chances are

your calling… is calling out to you.

Body Image: Everyone Thinks They're Too (Fill in the Blank)

When I was a sophomore, the soccer coach made us stand on a scale, and if you weighed more than a certain amount, you had to do extra running after practice. I was always in that group....

I never went to the swimming pool with the other kids; I rarely wore a bathing suit, and when I did, I put a T-shirt over it. It wasn't until I was a freshman in college that I got comfortable with my body....

I came to understand that this is who I am, and this is what I'm working with, as the expression goes, and I'm comfortable with myself.

— Brandi Chastain

When I became a teenager, I experienced times when I felt insecure about my looks. I wished that my face were more attractive... and wished that I were slimmer....

During those years there were many times I wished that I could mix and match body parts with someone else.... Over time, my physical features all caught up with one another and everything balanced out. As that happened, I started to come into my own and grow comfortable in my skin. At some point it just dawned on me that this is the body God gave me and I love and appreciate it no matter what.

— Serena Williams

Thirteen Things I Don't Want You to Do

Don't ~ stress out about things you have no control over.
Sometimes what is... just is.

Don't ~ waste your days in emotional disarray over a negative
situation that you *can* be in control of. (Remember, you
always have *at least* three options: move on; stay where you
are and just deal with it; or turn a negative situation into a
positive one.)

Don't ~ try to fit in with the "right" crowd when it
feels too forced. The best friendships are the ones
that are natural and easy and comfortable and kind.
Find one of those.

Don't ~ be a part of prejudice against anyone. Be
color-blind, and be open-minded to the millions
who have diverse beliefs and varying backgrounds.

Don't ~ worry about your future. It will unfold slowly enough
and give you plenty of time to help you decide... all the
where's and when's and why's.

Don't ~ feel like you have to put up with people who
are rude or obnoxious. Always take the higher ground when
you can, but if you need a release, take comfort
in quietly thinking to yourself, "I'm really glad I'm not
you..." and leave it at that.

Don't ~ forget, though, that some people have emotional or
physical things going on beneath the surface, and if we
knew what they were, we'd cut them a lot more slack.

Don't ~ ever forget that reckless behavior and cars are a deadly mix. People forget that every year, and when they do, it's often the last thing they'll ever forget.

Don't ~ be afraid to ask for advice. There are people who love you and care about you and would love to help you in any way they can. Be brave... and ask.

Don't ~ be obsessive about your body and your looks. You're growing and changing and you are a work in progress and a miracle in the making. The simple truth in the looks department is — some people are always going to seem better and others will always seem worse. It's okay. We're all different. That's pretty much the way the world works.

Don't ~ stop there: it's the same with money. There are the have-nots, the have-a-lots, and everybody in between. When your perspective gets lost and you're fretting about not having something "everyone else" has, remember, some can't afford the cost of anything.

Don't ~ let cynical people transfer their cynicism off on you. In spite of all its problems, it is still a pretty amazing world and there are lots of truly wonderful people spinning around on this planet.

And don't ~ ever forget: the teen years can definitely be challenging, but if you work it right... they're also some of the most memorable, and most fun,
    and most amazing times of life.

To put the world in order, we
must first put the nation in
order; to put the nation in
order, we must first put the
family in order; to put the
family in order, we must
cultivate our personal life;
and to cultivate our personal
life, we must first set our
hearts right.

— Confucius

Wherever I go, whatever I end up doing,
I'll always be the girl...
doing her best to make it happen.

— Picabo Street

It's Amazing… What Having a Healthy Point of View Can Do

I developed my escape routines like everybody else.…
At the age of fourteen — I would head off alone to
places where the steep hills came right down near
the road. I climbed dusty trails and boulder-filled
avalanche chutes up to the high places. The cool
mountain air was a blessed contrast to the overheated
atmosphere of home. I would propel my body upward,
making a mental pact with myself that if I could just
get to the top of the ridge or the peak, all the
anxiety that consumed me would fall away. It usually
worked, too. Arriving at the top, with my lungs and
thighs burning, I would look out and feel things
start to sort themselves out, fall into perspective.

— Mariel Hemingway

Rare Air

I want you to live by your own light
and shine by your own star. I want you
to envision the gift that you are.

Rise Above It

There will always be tough times and difficult days in our lives. It seems like some things weren't meant to be, and some plans just weren't meant to work out. There will always be disappointments to deal with, but there will be so many special blessings, too.

All that is asked of any of us is to try and rise above our problems. Let life show you new ways of doing things. Let it bring you new discoveries. Let it show you how to aim for the stars. Let it help you reach out to be all that you are.

It's a pretty simple rule: the more you give... the more you get back. And the more you do that, the more you'll love it.

You're a wonderful person who deserves to have a beautiful life. And if difficulty ever comes along, I know... that you can rise above it.

Inspired Reading

I had a very special teacher in high school many years ago whose husband unexpectedly and suddenly died of a heart attack. About a week after his death, she shared some of her insight with a classroom of students. As the late afternoon sunlight came streaming in through the classroom windows and the class was nearly over, she moved a few things aside on the edge of her desk and sat down there.

With a gentle look of reflection on her face, she paused and said, "Before class is over, I would like to share with all of you a thought that is unrelated to class, but which I feel is very important. Each of us is put here on earth to learn, share, love, appreciate, and give of ourselves. None of us knows when this fantastic experience will end. It can be taken away at any moment. Perhaps this is the 'powers that be' way of telling us that we must make the most out of every single day."

Her eyes beginning to water, she went on, "So I would like you all to make me a promise. From now on, on your way to school, or on your way home, find something beautiful to notice. It doesn't have to be something you see; it could be a scent — perhaps of freshly baked bread wafting out of someone's house, or it could be the sound of the breeze... or the way the morning light catches the autumn leaf as it falls gently to the ground.

"Please look for these things and cherish them. For, although it may sound trite to some, these things are the 'stuff' of life. The little things we are put here on earth to enjoy. The things we often take for granted. We must make it important to notice them, for at any time... it can all be taken away."

The class was completely quiet. We all picked up our books and filed out of the room silently. That afternoon, I noticed more things on my way home from school than I had that whole semester.

Every once in a while, I think of that teacher and remember what an impression she made on all of us, and I try to appreciate all of those things that sometimes we all overlook. Take notice of something special you see... today. Go barefoot. Or walk on the beach at sunset. Stop off on the way home... to get a double-dip ice-cream cone.

For as we get older, it is not the things we did that we often regret, but the things we didn't do.

— Anonymous

Life is not measured by the number of breaths we take, but by the moments that take our breath away.

— Anonymous

Don't Ever Stop
Dreaming Your Dreams

Don't ever try to understand everything —
some things will just never make sense.
Don't ever be reluctant
    to show your feelings —
    when you're happy, give in to it!
    When you're not, live with it.
Don't ever be afraid to try to
    make things better —
    you might be surprised at the results.
Don't ever take the weight of the world
    on your shoulders...
Don't ever feel threatened by the future —
    take life one day at a time.

Don't ever feel guilty about the past —
    what's done is done. Learn from any
    mistakes you might have made.
Don't ever feel that you are alone —
    there is always somebody there for you
    to reach out to.
Don't ever forget that you can achieve
    so many of the things you can imagine —
    imagine that! It's not as hard as it seems.
Don't ever stop loving,
        don't ever stop believing,
            don't ever stop dreaming your dreams.

---

*The choice was always mine... Do you walk away from
your dreams because everything just feels too difficult?
Or do you find another way?*

— Terrell Owens

The Discovery Process

This is a magnificent journey you're on. Don't be afraid to explore unfamiliar territory. If you do happen to get lost, you will stumble across some of the most interesting discoveries you'll ever make. Wander down roads you've never taken before or ones you'll never chance upon again. Life isn't a travel guide to follow...

It's an adventure to undertake.

It is in the journey that you learn the most about yourself. That self-knowledge will help you not only along the way but also beyond, because of course, as you reach one goal, you gain confidence to aspire to the next.

— Mia Hamm

If we did all the things we are capable of doing, we would literally astound ourselves.

— Thomas A. Edison

I discovered at an early age that most of the differences between average and top people could be explained in three words. The top people did what was expected of them — and then some. They were thoughtful of others and considerate and kind — and then some.

They met their obligations and responsibilities fairly and squarely — and then some. They were good friends to their friends, and could be counted on — and then some.

— Anonymous

Summer Dogs

You don't need a certain number of friends,
only a number of friends you can be certain of.

— *Anonymous*

Social... Security

Some of the luckiest people in the world are those who have a wonderful friend to share life with...

A friend who cares and who shares the gifts of smiles and closeness and companionship. Someone with whom you have so much in common. Somebody who's a precious part of the best memories you'll ever make. A special friend. A true friend. One to confide in, one who never lets you down, and one who always understands. A friend who is simply amazing because their heart is so big, their soul is so beautiful, and because everything about them inspires everything that is good about you.

Not using good judgment in choosing your friends and hanging out with the wrong crowd can undermine all the good things you've done and great decisions you've made.

— Serena Williams

Stand for Something
or You'll Fall for Anything

I wanted everybody to love *me* so badly that for years
I let other people's plans and priorities run my life.
I allowed others to take from me without giving back,
to goad or guilt me into solving their problems, to
use me for their own ends, all because I was scared
of losing their love and approval....

People who *really* love you don't put conditions on
their feelings. They don't say, "I'll love you as long
as you do what I want you to." Or, "I'll love you on
the condition you continue to please me." They say,
"I love you" — period, end of sentence.

Since I reached this understanding, it's impossible to
overstate how different my life is. How much richer
and fuller and *easier*. While I'm not insensitive to
the needs and wants of others, I have learned how
crucial it is to honor my own.

— Patti LaBelle

Do what you have to do to maintain your honor, your dignity, and your integrity. They are so important. Trust me on this one.

The way it works is like this: you are granted those qualities from the very beginning. They are yours to protect and treasure. You have them as long as you do nothing to diminish them. And you can do wonderful things that will add immeasurably to those qualities over the course of your life. If you possess them, you will always be held in high esteem. You will have a clear conscience, you will have a steady supply of serenity, and you will continue to pass one of life's most important tests.

But like any other priceless treasures, you can also lose them. Sometimes in a hurry. And it's not like they vanish forever, but once they're gone, you have to work ten times as hard to get them back. The way I see it is…

Better to just hold on to them from the start. Honor and dignity and integrity. Those three things will bless your days more than my words can even begin to say.

Wish List

I want you to be happy. I want you to fill your heart with feelings of wonder and I want you to be full of courage and hope. I want you to have the type of friendship that is a treasure — and the kind of life that is beautiful forever. I wish you contentment: the sweet, quiet, inner kind that comes around and never goes away.

I want you to have hopes and have them all come true. I want you to make the most of this moment in time. I want you to have a real understanding of how unique and rare you truly are. I want to remind you that the sun may disappear for a while, but it never forgets to shine. I want you to have faith.

May you have feelings that are shared from heart to heart, simple pleasures amidst this complex world, and wonderful goals that are within your grasp. May the words you listen to say the things you need to hear. And may a cheerful face lovingly look back at you when you happen to glance in the mirror.

I wish you the insight to see your inner and outer beauty. I wish you sweet dreams. I want you to have times when you feel like singing and dancing and laughing out loud. I want you to be able to make yourself proud.

Make choices that keep the peace and make you feel proud of how you represent yourself.

— Venus Williams

24 Things to Always Remember... and One Thing to Never Forget

Your presence is a present to the world.
You're unique and one of a kind.
Your life can be what you want it to be.
Take the days just one at a time.

Count your blessings, not your troubles.
You'll make it through whatever comes along.
Within you are so many answers.
Understand, have courage, be strong.

Don't put limits on yourself.
So many dreams are waiting to be realized.
Decisions are too important to leave to chance.
Reach for your peak, your goal, your prize.

Nothing wastes more energy than worrying.
The longer one carries a problem,
    the heavier it gets.
Don't take things too seriously.
Live a life of serenity, not a life of regrets.

Remember that a little love goes a long way.
Remember that a lot... goes forever.
Remember that friendship is a wise investment.
Life's treasures are people... together.

Realize that it's never too late.
Do ordinary things in an extraordinary way.
Have health and hope and happiness.
Take the time to wish upon a star.

And don't ever forget...
    for even a day... how very special you are.

Still Water

Even if you can't just snap your fingers and make a dream come true, you can travel in the direction of your dream, every single day, and you can keep shortening the distance between the two of you.

Current Events

I want this moment in time
to absolutely shine for you.

In your life, which is
so precious to me,
may troubles, worries,
and problems
never linger; may they
only make you that much
stronger and able and wise.

And may you rise today
with sunlight in your heart,
success in your path,
answers to your prayers,
and that smile
    that I love to see
always there… in your eyes.

Advice for Riding
on Roller Coasters

Problems and predicaments come
to us all. There's no sign saying,
"You must be this tall..." to ride
on the emotional roller coasters
that take so many of us for a spin.

Unfortunately, there are times
when others want us to share the
ride with them, and there are
circumstances that cause us to be
passengers whether we like it or not.

The fortunate thing about roller
coasters is... we can always choose
to get off at the next stop.

If you have troubles, secrets you keep inside, problems that are getting to be more of a problem, and deep concerns...

You need to get help and learn the best way out and around and through. And you need to realize that you're not alone — other people are right there with you.

> *Move ahead of every worry. Move beyond any sorrows. Have yourself a wealth of beautiful tomorrows.*

A Valuable Life Lesson

When I was growing up, my grandmother told me that people were going to talk about me and get in my business, and there was nothing I could do about this. They weren't going to understand my ways, so I should just accept it....

You've got to be very strong, she insisted, and make your own decisions, because nobody else can do that for you. You've got to know the difference between right and wrong and always figure out which side of that line you're standing on....

The older I've gotten, the more I've been surrounded by temptation, especially when I started to find success in pro football. Everywhere I turned, there was a chance to go astray, with drugs or women or booze or violence... or many other things. Whenever I was standing at the crossroads, I thought about my grandmother, and she helped me through.

— Terrell Owens

Carry the sun inside you, and reach out
for the dreams that guide you.
You have everything you need to take you
where you want to go.
You have abilities and talents and attributes
that belong to you alone, and you have
what it takes to make your path of
success... lead to happiness.
You are a special person, and you have a future
that is in the best of hands. And you need
to remember: if you have plans you want to
act on and dreams you've always wanted to
come true...

You have what it takes, because...

You have you.

> *Your body needs every edge it can get...*
> *That means eating good foods... and of course,*
> *avoiding drugs, alcohol, and cigarettes.*
> — *Mia Hamm*

This Is a Time of Wonderful Possibilities

New journeys await you. Decisions lie ahead, wondering... What will you do? Where will you go? How will you choose when the choices are yours?

Remember that good decisions come back to bless you, over and over again. Work for the ability to choose wisely, to prosper, to succeed. Listen with your heart as well as your head, to the glimmers of truth that provide advice and inspiration to the hours of your days. And let those truths take you to beautiful places.

Touch the sky, and in your reach, believe, achieve, and aspire.

I hope your tomorrows take you to the summit of your goals, and your joys take you even higher.

When I reflect now, I can see that all these lessons I learned... are truths my mother struggled to teach me....

Stop worrying about what other people think of you.
Be willing to take risks.
Failing doesn't hurt. Not trying does.
You can make an impression on someone
    without having to win.
Listen to your heart.
Stand up for what you believe in.

— Clay Aiken

If you accept the expectations of others, especially negative expectations, then you never will change the outcome.... That was the attitude I had ever since I was cut from the varsity team in high school. That attitude became a part of me.

— Michael Jordan

Rush Hour

Remember that some of the secret joys
of living are not found by rushing from
point A to point B, but by inventing
some imaginary letters along the way.

Getting from Here to There

Tomorrow is a beautiful road
that will take you right where
you want to go...

If you spend today
walking away from worry
    and moving toward serenity;
leaving behind conflict
    and traveling toward solutions;
and parting with emptiness
    and finding fulfillment.

If you can do what works for you,
your present will be happier
and your path will be smoother.

And best of all?
    You'll be taking a step
    into a beautiful future.

Things That Are Going to Happen in Your Life... (If They Haven't Already)

- You will never have all the answers. But you'll have a lot of intriguing questions, and the older and wiser you get, the more things will sort themselves out.
- You will be concerned about your future, wonder what's to come, and be uncertain how you'll manage.
- You will manage. As a matter of fact, you'll succeed.
- You will underestimate yourself. There are limits on how far you can go, but you'll never know what they are until you've reached out to achieve your very best.
- There will be times when your ego gets in the way; times when it would be infinitely better for it to get completely out of the way. (This takes some doing.)
- You will learn that accountability accounts for a lot.
- You will discover that the golden rule is amazing; the more you use it, the brighter your life shines.
- You will definitely fall in love. More than once.
- One day, your heart is going to be so broken that you'll wonder if you'll ever fall in love again.
- But you will. One day. Some day. For keeps.
- You'll learn the wisdom behind the saying, "It's nice to be important, but it's more important to be nice."
- You will learn that everyone has an agenda.
- People will surprise you... in good ways and bad.
- Some people who seem to be terrific will turn out to be sadly disappointing.

- Some people you never imagined as anything will turn out to be wonderful people you can't imagine ever being without.
- You will have friendships you will treasure forever.
- You will experience life's immense joys and deep sorrows.
- You will make memories you wouldn't trade for anything.
- You will have remembrances you'd just as soon forget.
- You will have people in your life who will die or become disabled because of alcohol or drug-related issues.
  (I lost two dear friends in this manner, one girl, one boy, just after my teenage years. I wish they had made better choices; I wish they were still here.)
- You will be in difficult situations yourself, in places you'd rather not be, or with others jeopardizing your well-being.
- You will come out of it just fine, as long as you do whatever it takes to get yourself into a better place and put control of the situation in your hands, not at the whim of someone else.
- You will eventually, proudly, happily discover that all the good things you can do… having the right attitude (one that helps you deal with it when things are bad, and one that makes good days into great ones); having a strong belief in your abilities; making good choices and responsible decisions; all those good things you can do will pay huge dividends.
- You'll see. Your prayers will be heard.
- Your karma will kick in.
- The sacrifices you made will be repaid.
- And the good work will have all been worth it.

Hope You Get Over It

Your own special horizon is out
there now — your goal, your hope,
your special wish, just waiting to get
a visit from you.

What It Takes

It takes a lot to set your
sights on a distant horizon
and to keep on reaching for
your goals. It takes a lot...
of courage and hard work,
believing and achieving,
patience and perseverance,
inner strength and gentle
hope. It takes a lot of giving
it your best and doing the
fantastic things you do.

But most of all...

It takes someone as
wonderful as
you.

Your Life Story

Each day brings with it the
miracle of a new beginning.
Many of the moments ahead
will be marvelously disguised
as ordinary days, but each one
of us has the chance to make
something extraordinary out
of them.

> *Enjoy the day. There will be another one tomorrow.*
> *Enjoy life for the sake of life.*
>
> — *Michael Jordan*

Each day is a blank page in the diary of your life. And there is something special you need to remember in order to turn your life story into the treasure it deserves to be.

This is how it works...

Follow your dreams. Work hard. Be kind. This is all anyone could ever ask: do what you can to make the door open on a day that is filled with inspiration in some special way.

Remember: Goodness will be rewarded. Smiles will pay you back. Have fun. Find strength. Be truthful. Have faith. Don't focus on anything you lack.

Realize that people are the treasures in life, and happiness is the real wealth. Have a diary that describes how you are doing your best, and...

The rest will take care of itself.

My daily mission is to...
become a better decision maker.
— Brandi Chastain

Red Boat

I want everything to work out for you
just the way you want it to.

I Wish for You

Happiness. Deep down within.
Serenity. With each sunrise.
Success. In each facet of your life.
Close and caring friends.
Love. That never ends.

Special memories. Of all
    the yesterdays.
A bright today. With so much
    to be thankful for.
A path. That leads to
    beautiful tomorrows.

Dreams. That do their best to come true.
And appreciation. Of all the wonderful
       things about you.

ACKNOWLEDGMENTS

We gratefully acknowledge the permission granted by the following authors, publishers, and authors' representatives to reprint poems or excerpts from their publications.

Crown Books, a division of Random House, Inc., for "I have created the opportunity...," "If you accept the expectations...," and "Enjoy the day..." from FOR THE LOVE OF THE GAME by Michael Jordan. Copyright © 1998 by Michael Jordan. All rights reserved.

HarperCollins Publishers for "One of the most important parts...," "It is in the journey...," and "Your body needs..." from GO FOR THE GOAL by Mia Hamm and Aaron Heifetz. Copyright © 1999 by Mia Hamm. All rights reserved. And for "When I was a sophomore..." and "My daily mission..." from IT'S NOT ABOUT THE BRA by Brandi Chastain. Copyright © 2004 by Brandi Chastain. All rights reserved.

G.P. Putnam's Sons, a division of Penguin Group (USA), Inc., for "There was social pressure..." from IT'S NOT ABOUT THE BIKE by Lance Armstrong. Copyright © 2000 by Lance Armstrong. All rights reserved.

Random House, Inc., for "So much has happened since..." and "When I reflect now..." from LEARNING TO SING by Clay Aiken and Allison Glock. Copyright © 2004 by Clay Aiken. All rights reserved.

Houghton Mifflin Company for "Serena and I believe there's nothing...," "Make choices that keep...," "When I became a teenager...," and "Not using good judgment..." from SERVING FROM THE HIP: 10 RULES FOR LIVING, LOVING AND WINNING by Venus Williams and Serena Williams. Text copyright © 2005 by Venus Williams and Serena Williams. Reprinted by permission. All rights reserved.

The McGraw-Hill Companies for "Get... involved in as many..." and "Wherever I go, whatever I end up..." from PICABO: NOTHING TO HIDE by Picabo Street. Copyright © 2002 by Picabo Street. All rights reserved.

Simon & Schuster for "I developed my escape routines..." from FINDING MY BALANCE by Mariel Hemingway. Copyright © 2003 by Fox Creek Productions f/s/o Mariel Hemingway. All rights reserved. And for "The choice was always mine..." and "When I was growing up..." from CATCH THIS! by Terrell Owens with Stephen Singular. Copyright © 2004 by Terrell Owens and Stephen Singular. All rights reserved.

Warner Books, Inc., for "I wanted everybody to love me..." from PATTI'S PEARLS by Patti LaBelle. Copyright © 2001 by Patti LaBelle and Laura Randolph Lancaster. Reprinted by permission of Warner Books, Inc. All rights reserved.

A careful effort has been made to trace the ownership of selections used in this anthology in order to obtain permission to reprint copyrighted material and give proper credit to the copyright owners. If any error or omission has occurred, it is completely inadvertent, and we would like to make corrections in future editions provided that written notification is made to the publisher:

BLUE MOUNTAIN ARTS, INC., P.O. Box 4549, Boulder, Colorado 80306.